100 Facts on British History

100 facts on British History

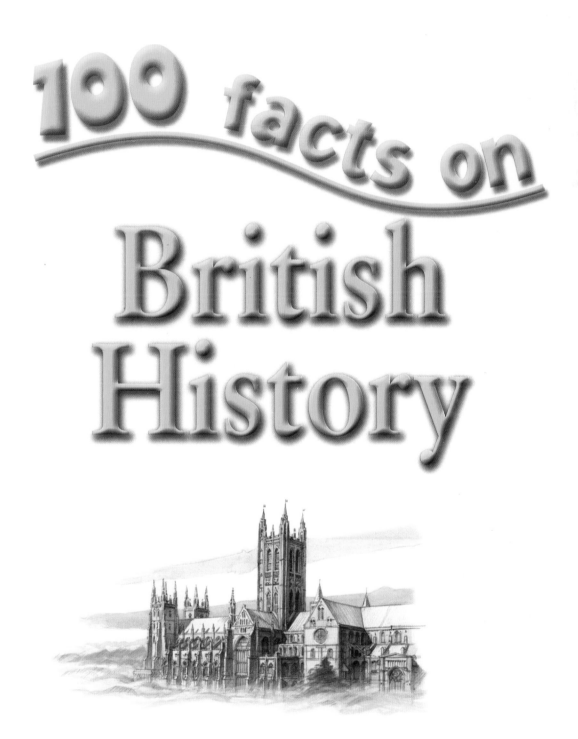

Philip Steele

Consultant: Fiona Macdonald

MiLes KeLLy PUBLISHING

First published in 2008 by Miles Kelly Publishing Ltd
Bardfield Centre, Great Bardfield, Essex, CM7 4SL

This material is also available in hardback and flexiback

2 4 6 8 10 9 7 5 3 1

Editorial Director Belinda Gallagher
Art Director Jo Brewer
Editorial Assistant Carly Blake
Volume Designer John Christopher, White Design
Copy Editor Sarah Ridley
Proofreader Margaret Berrill
Indexer Jane Parker
Reprographics Anthony Cambray, Liberty Newton, Ian Paulyn
Production Manager Elizabeth Brunwin

ISBN 978-1-84236-960-9

Printed in China

British Library Cataloguing-in-Publication Data
A catalogue record for this book is available from the British Library

ACKNOWLEDGEMENTS
The publishers would like to thank the following artists
who have contributed to this book:
Julie Banyard/Steve Caldwell/Peter Dennis/Mike Foster (Maltings Partnership)
Terry Gabbey/Luigi Galante/Sally Holmes/Richard Hook/John James
Kevin Maddison/Janos Marffy/Alessandro Menchi/Terry Riley/Pete Roberts
Martin Sanders/Peter Sarson/Rob Sheffield/Rudi Vizi/Steve Weston/Mike White
Cartoons by Mark Davis at Mackerel
Cover artwork by Mike Saunders

www.mileskelly.net
info@mileskelly.net

www.factsforprojects.com

Contents

In the beginning

1 **Human beings like us were living in Great Britain about 37,000 years ago.** They hunted animals, caught fish and gathered plants they could eat. They used simple tools and weapons made of stone and wood. Britain was not an island then, but part of mainland Europe. The weather was often very cold and the land became covered in ice for long periods of time. The last of these ice ages ended about 10,000 years ago. As the weather became warmer, the ice melted and the sea level rose. Britain became an island.

▶ As the last ice age ended and the climate became warmer, bands of hunters moved into new woodlands and wetlands. As well as deer, fish and shellfish were important food sources.

Stone and bronze

▼ Animals didn't just provide meat for food. Their skins were scraped clean with flint tools and then sewn together using bone needles to make clothing and tents.

2 By 6000BC, hunters in Britain had become skilled at making tools and weapons such as needles, fish hooks and harpoons. They hunted deer, boar and wild oxen in the oak forests. They used animal skins to make clothes and coverings for shelters.

▶ Careful chipping could turn a flint into a razor-sharp tool or weapon.

3 Flint was an excellent stone for making tools. It could be chipped and flaked until it was razor-sharp, like glass. The flints lay buried in chalk, so miners had to dig deep, as far as 10 metres down, to reach the best ones. The miners dug the flints out using deer antlers as picks.

▲ The skeletons of flint miners have been found buried in flint mines.

▲ Stone hand mills, or querns, were used for grinding wheat. The central hole was filled with grain and then the top stone was turned, or ground, against the bottom one. Flour spilled out between the stones.

4 Farming had reached the British Isles by about 4000BC. Villagers learned to raise sheep and goats. They grew wheat, which they harvested with stone tools. Then they ground the grain into flour. The bread may have been gritty and the animals may have been thin and bony, but it was easier than hunting!

▶ Molten (hot, liquid) bronze could be poured into stone moulds. The mould was smeared with soot and grease to give a smooth finish. When the bronze had cooled and hardened, the mould was knocked away.

5 Metal tools and weapons were better than stone ones. Copper was used in Britain by 2500BC. About 600 to 700 years later, people discovered how mixing copper with tin made a tough metal mixture, or alloy, called bronze.

I DON'T BELIEVE IT!

Some of the pillars at Stonehenge weighed as much as 20 elephants! People hauled them all the way from southwest Wales, a distance of over 215 kilometres.

6 Between 3000BC and 1500BC, massive pillars of stone were used to create a circle at Stonehenge in southern England. The stones were placed so that they lined up with the rising and setting Sun. It is thought that people used Stonehenge to study the Sun, Moon and stars, as well as to observe the seasons. People would have crowded into the circle on a midsummer morning to watch the rising of the Sun.

The ancient Celts

7 Around 600BC, small bands of warriors and traders from mainland Europe began to settle in parts of the British Isles. Many of them belonged to a people called the Celts. Those people already living in the British Isles slowly took on the Celtic way of life. They began to speak Celtic languages, too.

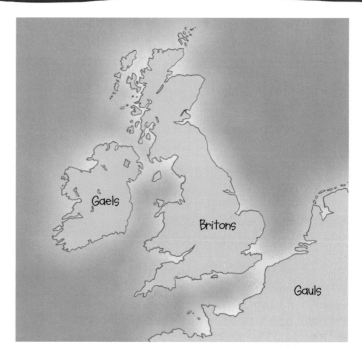

▲ The Celts gradually brought their way of life to many parts of Europe. The three main groups in the northwest of Europe were the Gauls of France, the Gaels of Ireland and the Britons of Great Britain.

8 The ancient Celts were famous for being show-offs. Celtic warriors sometimes wore their hair in spikes, tattooed their skin and wore heavy gold jewellery. Unlike most men in Europe at that time, they wore trousers beneath a short tunic. Women wore long dresses of wool or linen and used mirrors of polished bronze.

▶ The Celts made beautiful gold bracelets, such as this, and rings and brooches.

MAKE CELTIC COINS

You will need:

coins   heavy card   silver/gold paint
black felt-tip pen   scissors

1. Draw circles around modern coins onto heavy card.
2. Cut out the circles and paint them silver or gold.
3. When the paint is dry, draw your own designs with a black felt-tip pen. Celtic coins were decorated with horses, the heads of gods, or moons and stars.

9 **The safest place to be when war broke out was on top of a hill or on a headland by the coast.** These places could easily be defended from attack with ditches and high wooden fences. Ancient Celts often used hill forts like these. The Celts were great fighters and cattle raiders. They used chariots and fought with long swords.

▶ This great hill fort was at Maiden Castle in Dorset, England. It was protected by timber fences and banks of earth.

Timber fence

Settlement

Bank of earth

10 **The Celts were first-rate metal workers.** They knew all about iron. In fact iron was such a hard, useful metal that people who had not seen it before thought it must be magic. Some people still nail iron horseshoes onto doors for good luck.

▶ A smoky hearth was the centre of every Celtic round house.

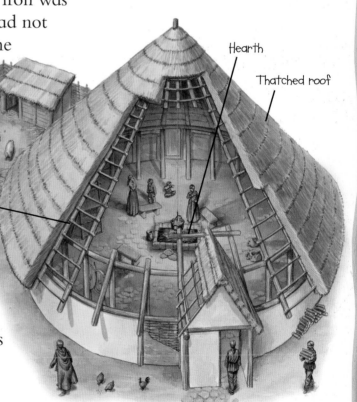

Hearth

Thatched roof

Timber poles

11 **Many British Celts lived in villages, in large round houses.** The walls were made of timber and clay, or stone. Inside each house was a fire. The smoke rose through a hole in the thatched roof. The Celts were farmers and blacksmiths and enjoyed hunting too. Their priests and lawmakers were called druids.

Roman Britain

12 **An army of 10,000 Roman soldiers landed in England in 55BC.** They were led by a general, Julius Caesar. He had already defeated the Gauls in France. However, the landing was not a success and the Romans returned to Gaul. In 54BC the Romans came back with 27,000 soldiers. They marched north to the River Thames and forced the people there to pay money to Rome.

◄ Roman coins are still found in Britain today.

13 **The Romans returned yet again in AD43 and this time they stayed.** They conquered all of Britain except for the north of Scotland, where they built the Antonine Wall to keep the Highlanders out. In AD122, the Roman's built Hadrian's Wall. This was the northern border of an empire that stretched from Spain, to North Africa and the Black Sea.

▲ The Roman name for Britain was Britannia. This map shows key places, roads and walls in Roman Britain.

14 **In AD60 there was a bloody revolt against Roman rule, led by a queen called Boudicca.** She burned down Roman towns. When her warriors were defeated, she killed herself in despair. Rich Britons now learned to live like Romans. Poorer Britons carried on farming and trading, much as they always had done.

▶ Boudicca led her armies to war against Rome and burned down London.

15

The Romans liked their comforts.
They built public baths where people could
have a cold or hot dip, a
work-out or a massage.
Rich people lived in
luxurious country-houses
called villas. These even
had under-the-floor
central heating.

◀ Floors were often decorated
with tile pictures called mosaics.

I DON'T BELIEVE IT!

The Romans' secret weapon of
war was ... a tortoise! 'Tortoise'
was the name given to a group of
soldiers who crouched under linking
shields to attack a hill fort. Enemy
spears just bounced off the top and
sides of the tortoise's 'shell'.

16

**Roman soldiers began to leave Britain in
AD401.** Many parts of the great empire were now under
attack. In Britain there were rebellions. Pirates sailed the
seas. The Irish attacked western shores. The city of Rome
itself was captured by German warriors in AD476.

17

**The Romans built long, straight roads
from one town to the next.** They were built
using layers of sand and gravel, paved with stone.
In fact, there were no better roads in Britain
until the 1800s.

Carts and horses
travelled the roads

Stone-paved surface

Roads were built with
layers of sand and gravel

▲ Roman armies could march along
the straight roads at high speed.

The Anglo-Saxons

▲ This Anglo-Saxon helmet dates from about AD625.

18 During the last days of the Roman Empire, raiders from northern Germany began to attack eastern Britain. More and more of them landed in the 400s and 500s. They belonged to various peoples known as Angles, Saxons, Jutes and Frisians. We call them all Anglo-Saxons. Their speech became the English language, mixed with Celtic and Latin.

▶ The Anglo-Saxons slowly conquered the southern and eastern lands of the British Celts. Armed warriors may have carried a long knife called a sax.

Sax

19 The invaders carried swords, axes and long knives. They burned down Celtic villages and old Roman towns and set up many small kingdoms. They built small villages of rectangular thatched houses and lived by farming and fishing.

▲ It took many years for the Anglo-Saxons to conquer much of the area now known as England. They divided it into many separate kingdoms.

20 The first Christians in Britain were Romans and Britons. The Anglo-Saxons still worshipped their own German gods such as Woden, god of war and wisdom. Then in 597 a monk called St Augustine set off from Rome to preach about Christ. He built a cathedral at Canterbury, in Kent.

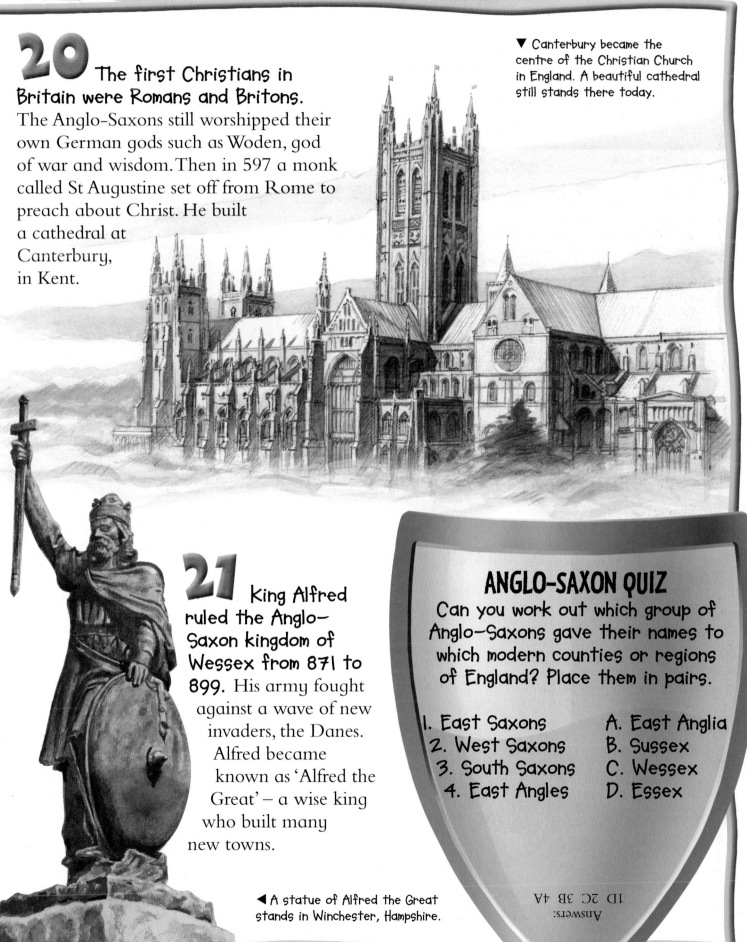

▼ Canterbury became the centre of the Christian Church in England. A beautiful cathedral still stands there today.

21 King Alfred ruled the Anglo-Saxon kingdom of Wessex from 871 to 899. His army fought against a wave of new invaders, the Danes. Alfred became known as 'Alfred the Great' – a wise king who built many new towns.

◀ A statue of Alfred the Great stands in Winchester, Hampshire.

ANGLO-SAXON QUIZ
Can you work out which group of Anglo-Saxons gave their names to which modern counties or regions of England? Place them in pairs.

1. East Saxons   A. East Anglia
2. West Saxons   B. Sussex
3. South Saxons   C. Wessex
4. East Angles   D. Essex

Answers:
1D 2C 3B 4A

The Irish

22 The Celtic-speaking people who lived in Ireland believed in the old Celtic gods. Then, in about 432, a British monk called St Patrick went to Ireland to preach the Christian faith. Over the next 200 years, monasteries were founded throughout Ireland. The monks made beautiful copies of the Bible by hand.

▲ About 1200 years ago, Irish monks made books by hand. They decorated their work with beautiful letters and pictures.

23 In the 700s and 800s, the Irish were some of the finest craftworkers in Europe. They made splendid brooches and cups of gold and silver, and were also famous for their stonework. The Irish were known as great storytellers, too.

24 In the 500s, an Irish monk called St Brendan is said to have sailed westwards to explore the lands around the Atlantic Ocean. Tales about his voyages tell of islands, whales and volcanoes.

MAKE AN IRISH BROOCH

You will need:

scissors   stiff card   safety pin
gold and silver paint or pens

1. Cut out a circle and a long pin shape from stiff card. Glue them together.

2. Colour one side gold with paint or a pen. Decorate with patterns as shown below.

5. Tape a safety pin on the back at the widest part of the brooch so that it can be worn.

25 **Ireland was divided into separate kingdoms.** Each ruler was supposed to recognize a High King as his chief, although the kings often quarrelled and fought with each other. In about 500, one northern group of Irish set up another kingdom called Dalriada, across the sea in western Scotland.

26 **Brian Ború became High King of all Ireland in 1002.** He fought many battles with other Irish kings. He also fought against invaders from Scandinavia, the Vikings. Brian Ború defeated all his enemies at Clontarf in 1014, but was murdered after the battle.

◄ The Battle of Clontarf marked the end of Viking power in Ireland.

The Vikings

27 The Vikings were pirates and raiders, traders, settlers, explorers and farmers. Some people called them Northmen or Danes, for their homeland was in Norway, Sweden and Denmark. Viking raiders began to attack the British Isles in 789 and were soon feared far and wide.

28 Viking longships were sleek, wooden vessels about 18 metres long. They had a single sail and could speed through the waves. The oars were manned by a crew of 30 or more. Ships like these carried Vikings far to the west, to Iceland, Greenland and North America.

29

Viking warriors attacked monasteries, villages and towns, carrying away treasure, cattle or slaves. They were armed with round shields, axes, swords and spears and wore helmets of leather or iron. Some spent the gold they robbed buying tunics made of tough iron rings, called mail.

30

In the 840s and 850s, Viking warriors began to settle in Britain and Ireland. They lived in villages and seaports and captured large towns such as York. They founded the city of Dublin in Ireland.

I DON'T BELIEVE IT!

Do you know what the word berserk means? To the Vikings it meant 'bearskin shirt', as worn by warriors who worked themselves up into a frenzy before going into battle. We still use the word today to describe someone who is violently angry.

31

Vikings fought against the Anglo-Saxons and soon controlled large areas of England. In 1016 England even had a Danish king called Cnut I. Vikings also ruled the Isle of Man and large areas of Scotland and Ireland.

◄ The Vikings were not just interested in raiding and stealing. They realized that the British Isles provided good farmland and safe areas for settlements.

The Welsh

32 The Anglo—Saxons did not settle in the land of the West Britons, although by 607 they had cut it off from the other Celtic lands to the north. They called this land Wales. In about 784, the Saxon king, Offa, built a massive wall of earth along the border as a defence against Welsh attacks. Offa's Dyke still stands today.

◄ Crosses on early Welsh churches were beautifully carved from stone.

▶ During the early Middle Ages, Wales was made up of several smaller kingdoms, each with its own ruler. These rulers were constantly fighting each other, trying to conquer the rest of Wales.

33 Wales and Cornwall had been centres of Christianity since Roman times. A Welsh priest called St David, who lived from 520 to 601, built new churches across the land.

34 Wales was divided into several kingdoms. These included Gwynedd, Powys, Dyfed and Ceredigion. One ruler, Hywel the Good, ended up controlling most of Wales. He began to make new laws that were used in Wales for over 500 years. He died in 950.

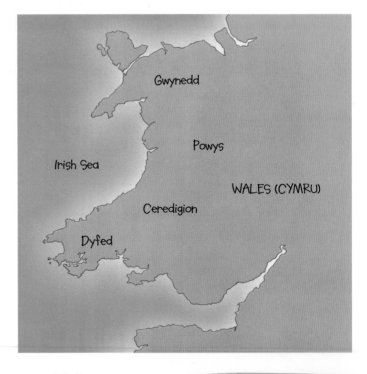

Gwynedd

Powys

Irish Sea

WALES (CYMRU)

Ceredigion

Dyfed

▲ Welsh warriors patrolled the lands to the west of Offa's Dyke. They sometimes raided parts of England for cattle and slaves.

35 Llywelyn the Great came to rule Gwynedd in 1194. He was a wise and strong ruler. He married Joan, the daughter of King John of England, but the two men became bitter enemies.

◀ This stone head is said to be a sculpture of Llywelyn the Great.

36 Llywelyn ap Gruffudd united all of Wales under his rule. He fought a long war against the English and was killed near Cilmeri in 1282. The English now ruled Wales. King Edward I declared that in future the eldest son of the English king would be the Prince of Wales.

I DON'T BELIEVE IT!

Legend says that on 1 March 640 St David was present at a battle between Christian soldiers from Wales and the non-Christian Saxons. On the battlefield it was hard to tell who was on which side. St David told his men to pull up leeks and wear them in their caps, as a badge. The leek is still an emblem of Wales today.

The Scots

37 In about 563 an Irish monk called Columcille, or Columba, founded a monastery on the Scottish island of Iona. He travelled all over Scotland and taught people about the Christian faith.

I DON'T BELIEVE IT!

In the days before printing, people had to copy books by hand. This was mostly done by monks. It is said that St Columba copied no fewer than 300 books himself!

38 Over the years the different parts of Scotland united as one country. The Scots and Picts joined together in 847 under the rule of Kenneth MacAlpin. By 1043 all the different peoples of Scotland belonged to the new kingdom as well, which was ruled by King Duncan I.

▶ Columba arrived on the Scottish island of Iona with a handful of companions. He converted many people to the Christian faith.

39
The Scottish kings had trouble controlling their border lands. Norwegians occupied islands and coasts in the north and west until the 1100s. After them, chieftains called the Lords of the Isles ruled much of the west. Along the southern border, war with England went on for hundreds of years.

40
Duncan I only ruled Scotland for six years. He was killed by a rival called Macbeth. Macbeth actually turned out to be a good king, but in 1057 Duncan's son, Malcolm, marched back into Scotland and killed Macbeth. Malcolm became king in 1058.

◀ Duncan I became king of Scotland in 1034. He was killed in battle by Macbeth.

▶ Margaret became Queen of Scotland aged 24. She brought many good changes to the country.

41
In 1070 Malcolm III was married in Dunfermline. His bride was an English lady who had been born in Hungary. Her name was Margaret. The new queen made the Scottish court a fine place. She founded many monasteries and the Church later made her a saint.

The Normans

42 An English king called Edward the Confessor died in 1066. Harold II became king after him, but no fewer than seven other people claimed that they should be king instead. One of these was William, Duke of Normandy. The Normans – Northmen – were descended from Vikings who had settled in France.

43 William crossed the English Channel with a fleet of ships. His army landed and met the English in a great battle near Hastings in Sussex. Axes crashed on shields, arrows whistled through the air, horses neighed. King Harold was killed and the Normans marched to London.

▶ The Norman army defeated the English at the Battle of Hastings in 1066.

44 William was crowned king of England in Westminster Abbey, London, on Christmas Day 1066. He built a stone fortress there, as part of the Tower of London. Soon William I controlled all England. He became known as William the Conqueror.

45 **The Normans created the Domesday Book.** In it they recorded the houses and lands in their new kingdom. People had to work for their new Norman lords and pay taxes. The Domesday Book helped the king keep track of everything.

Domesday Book

46 **The Normans attacked and settled in parts of Wales.** They also settled in the Lowlands of Scotland. By 1166 Norman knights were becoming involved in wars in Ireland and seizing land there, too.

47 **During the 1100s the kings of England kept close links with France.** They married into French families. King Henry II of England ruled an empire that stretched all the way to southwestern France.

NORMAN QUIZ
True or false?
1. The Normans were named after their first leader, Norman the Strong.
2. The kings of England spoke French after 1066.
3. William I became known as William the Wanderer.

Answers:
1. FALSE The word Normans comes from Northmen, meaning Vikings.
2. TRUE French was the language of the royal court until the 1300s.
3. FALSE He became known as William the Conqueror.

25

Castles and knights

48 The Normans began to build castles in Britain. These were a type of fortress in which people lived. They helped to control areas that had been conquered. The first Norman castles were made of wood, but before long they were made with thick stone walls and had towers. Water-filled ditches called moats surrounded them. Castles were built in Britain for 400 years.

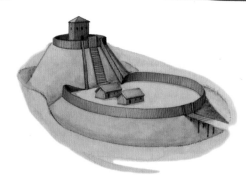

1000: a timber castle built on a mound

1150: a castle with a square stone tower, or keep

Helmet

Pauldron

Breastplate

Tasset

Cuisse

◀ By the 1400s knights wore armour of steel plates that covered the entire body. They no longer needed shields.

1300: a castle with many surrounding walls

I DON'T BELIEVE IT!

A suit of chain mail armour, as worn by a knight in the 1100s, weighed over 13 kilograms. Add to that weight the knight's great sword, axes and other weapons — and pity the poor warhorse!

49 From the Norman period onwards, the most important troops were mounted soldiers called knights. In battle, the knights were protected by armour. At first they wore chain mail. By the 1400s they wore plate armour that covered every part of the body, even the face.

50 Each noble family had its own badge called a coat-of-arms. This appeared on shields and flags and helped to show which knight was which during a battle. There were strict rules about the design of coats-of-arms, known as heraldry.

51 Knights liked to practise fighting in mock battles called tournaments. They showed off to the crowd and wore fancy armour. Even so, they often risked their lives.

▼ Knights engaging in foot combat wore heavy armour. Skill and speed were more important than strength.

52 In the great hall of the castle, lords and ladies feasted at grand banquets. There were many courses, with venison (deer meat), swan or goose, and all kinds of pies and puddings.

◄ A boar's head with all the trimmings was a popular dish at banquets.

Life in the Middle Ages

53 **The king had power over everyone.** If the nobles served him well, he gave them land and castles. Poor peasants had to work for the local lord, providing food and fighting services in return for land. It was a hard life and sometimes the peasants revolted (rebelled) in protest.

54 **Lords sometimes revolted against the king, too.** In England, lords forced King John to sign an agreement called Magna Carta in 1215. It said that even the king had to obey the laws of the land.

55 Towns were still quite small and were surrounded by high walls. The streets were narrow, muddy and smelly. Houses built of timber could catch fire all too easily.

56 All the Christians in western Europe now belonged to the Roman Church. Great stone cathedrals were built, soaring to the sky. People called pilgrims travelled far and wide to pray at holy sites, such as Canterbury Cathedral in Kent.

57 In 1348 a terrible disease called the Black Death arrived in the British Isles. It was a plague that was spread by rat fleas biting people. This disease killed many millions of people right across Asia and Europe.

▼ Towns were important centres of trade and local crafts. Knights and their squires on the way to tournaments would often stop to buy food and drink.

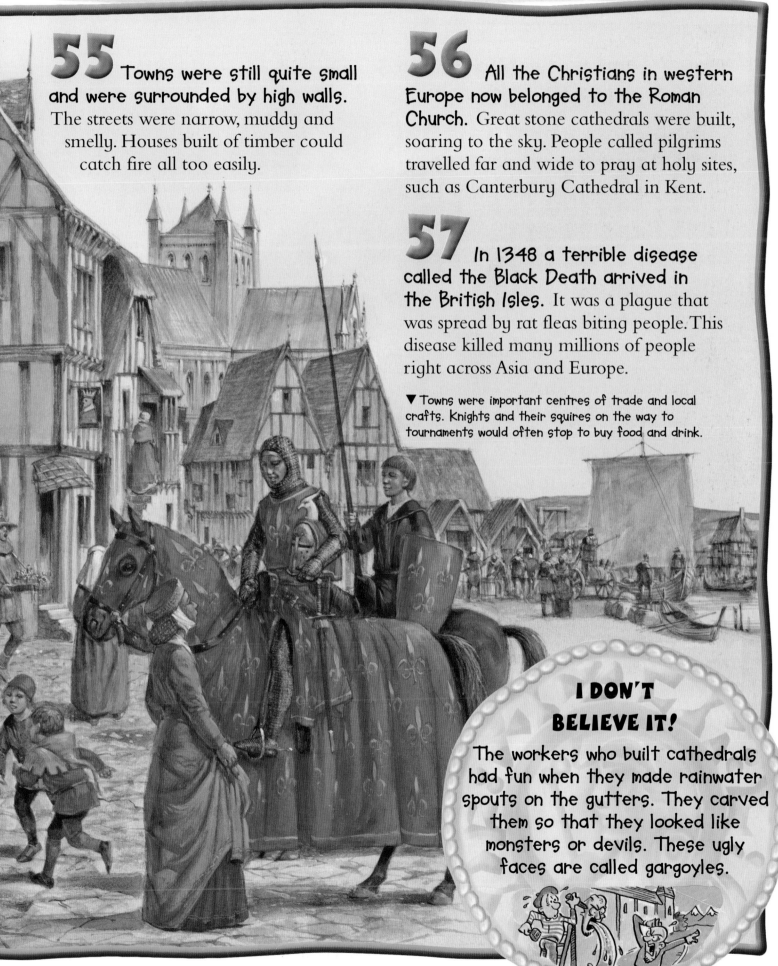

I DON'T BELIEVE IT!

The workers who built cathedrals had fun when they made rainwater spouts on the gutters. They carved them so that they looked like monsters or devils. These ugly faces are called gargoyles.

Battles and wars

58 During the Middle Ages Christian knights from all over Europe began a terrible series of wars against people of other faiths. Most of these 'Crusades' were fought between 1096 and 1291 against Muslims in the Near East. King Richard I of England, known as *Coeur de Lion* or 'Lion Heart', led the Third Crusade in 1190.

Christian knight

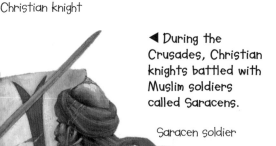

◀ During the Crusades, Christian knights battled with Muslim soldiers called Saracens.

Saracen soldier

59 The English and Scots were deadly enemies for many years. Scottish leaders included William Wallace and Robert Bruce. Bruce often despaired of victory. One day, whilst watching a spider try and try again to rebuild its web, he vowed to do the same. He defeated the English at Bannockburn in 1314.

60
The Welsh rose up against English rule in 1400. Their leader was called Owain Glyndwr. He made alliances with rebel English lords and with France. Welsh archers used the new longbow, a fearsome weapon, but the rising failed after 16 years of struggle.

61
The Hundred Years War did not last 100 years! It actually lasted longer – from 1337 to 1453. It was a series of wars between the English and the French. Henry V led the English to a great victory at Agincourt in 1415, but gradually England lost its lands in France.

English knight

Muslim archer

Scottish foot soldier

Welsh archer

▲ During the Middle Ages, soldiers wore different dress for battle. They also used various weapons. The English and Welsh both favoured the deadly longbow.

62
From 1455 to 1485, two families of English nobles fought for the throne in the Wars of the Roses. The badge of the House of Lancaster was a red rose, while the House of York had a white rose.

The red rose of Lancaster

The white rose of York

▶ Cannons such as this were hauled to the battlefields during the Wars of the Roses.

Tudors and Stewarts

63 **The Tudor family were of Welsh descent.** They ruled England and Wales after 1485 and also controlled a small part of Ireland, around Dublin. The first Tudor king, Henry VII, united England under his rule. The Tudor rulers and nobles liked to live in fine palaces rather than draughty castles.

64 **The Stewart family ruled Scotland.** Their greatest king was James IV. He built a fleet of ships and fine palaces, too. Musicians and poets came to his court. James was killed fighting the English in 1513.

65 **Henry VIII came to the English throne in 1509.** People had great hopes of him being a good king, but as he grew older he became selfish and jealous. He married six times. Two of his wives were beheaded!

▶ Henry VIII was a good dancer and musician. His court was often the scene of extravagant royal balls. Henry was also an intelligent and capable king who was very interested in education and religion.

66 When Henry VIII tried to divorce his first wife, he quarrelled with the Pope in Rome. To get his divorce, Henry cut ties with Rome and made himself Head of the Church in England.

67 During the 1500s people were arguing about religion, in the British Isles and all over Europe. The Roman Catholics supported the Pope, but the Protestants wanted to break away from the Church in Rome. King Edward VI of England was a Protestant, but he died young. His sister, Mary I, was a Roman Catholic. In the 1550s she ordered many Protestants to be burnt alive when they refused to give up their faith.

ROYAL QUIZ

True or false?
1. Henry VIII had three of his wives beheaded.
2. Henry VIII liked to write pop songs.
3. The Stewarts changed the spelling of their name.
4. Mary I of England was a Protestant.

Answers:
1. FALSE Two were beheaded.
2. TRUE He composed all kinds of music, including religious and popular songs. He loved dancing.
3. TRUE They later spelled the name with a 'u'—Stuart.
4. FALSE She was Catholic.

The Elizabethans

68 Elizabeth I, daughter of Henry VIII, came to the throne in 1558. She had her father's temper as well as his love of music, dancing and fine clothes. Unlike him, she never married. She was also a much wiser ruler than Henry. Elizabeth died in 1603, the last of the Tudors.

▶ Elizabeth I was greatly respected, and knew how to win public approval.

69 The English countryside was full of sheep in Tudor times. Merchants sold wool and cloth across Europe. Many parts of England became very wealthy.

70 Mary Stuart, Queen of Scots, fled to England in 1568. Scotland was going through troubled times. Although a cousin of Elizabeth, Mary was also a threat. In 1587 she was accused of plotting against Elizabeth and she was beheaded.

▲ The smaller, faster English ships defeated the mighty Spanish fleet, or Armada.

71 English seafarers were busy exploring. In 1577 to 1581 Sir Francis Drake sailed right round the world. By the 1600s, English people were settling along the coasts of North America. Their first settlement was called Virginia.

72 In 1588 Catholic Spain sent a fleet of ships (the Armada) to invade England. The Armada was attacked by English ships along the Channel and then scattered by storms.

◀ Shakespeare's plays were first performed in the Globe Theatre during the 1600s.

73 In the 1590s and 1600s, theatres became very popular in London. People crowded into them to see the plays of William Shakespeare.

Roundheads and Cavaliers

74 Elizabeth I died without having had children. The throne passed to James VI of Scotland, son of Mary, Queen of Scots. James now became James I of England as well. James proved to be an intelligent king who wrote about the dangers of tobacco and introduced a new English translation of the Bible.

▲ Charles I lost the Civil War and was beheaded in 1649.

75 In 1605, soldiers searching the cellars of the Houses of Parliament discovered barrels of gunpowder. A Catholic called Guy Fawkes along with 12 other men was accused of plotting to blow up the king and Parliament. The failure of the plot has been celebrated every 5th November since then, with bonfires and fireworks.

▼ The leaders of the Gunpowder Plot were tortured before being put to death.

76 James' son, Charles I, forced people to pay unfair taxes. Members of Parliament were so angry that they went to war with the king. The king's soldiers were called Cavaliers and the soldiers of Parliament were called Roundheads. The Roundheads won and Charles had his head chopped off.

77

In 1653 Parliament handed over power to a soldier called Oliver Cromwell. He ruled as Lord Protector for five years. Cromwell was supported by extreme Protestants, called Puritans.

78

In 1660 Parliament decided to have a king again. The son of the old king (Charles I) became Charles II. The Puritans took life and religion seriously and did not like dancing or the theatre. But Charles II did – people started having fun again!

▼ After the strict ways of the Puritans, people welcomed the more relaxed rule of Charles II.

I DON'T BELIEVE IT!

When he was a student at Cambridge, Oliver Cromwell was more famous as a football player than as a politician. Football was a very rough game in those days, without the rules we know today.

Plague and fire

79 **In 1665 the plague, or Black Death, returned to London.** Thousands died in the first few months. Carts came round the streets to collect the dead. City folk fled to the countryside – taking their deadly germs with them.

80 **In 1666 a spark from a fire set a bakery alight in Pudding Lane, London.** The fire spread through the city for five whole days, destroying over 13,000 timber-framed houses and St Paul's Cathedral. The city was rebuilt in stone. A new cathedral was designed by Sir Christopher Wren.

▼ Rat fleas spread the Black Death, but people did not know this. Red crosses painted on doors told people that plague was present in a house.

▼ The Great Fire of London was made worse by strong winds. About 80 percent of the old city was destroyed.

81 When Charles II died in 1685, his brother became King James II of England (James VII of Scotland). James was a Catholic and the Protestants were angry. They threw him off the throne. Instead, they made his daughter Queen Mary II. Her Protestant husband William, who already ruled the Netherlands, became king. William III and Mary II ruled jointly.

Mary II

William III

82 The 1600s and 1700s were lawless times. Highwaymen lay in wait on lonely heaths and held up travellers' coaches. Pirates sailed the seas, attacking and robbing ships.

83 Queen Anne was the last of the Stuarts. She ruled from 1701 to 1714. In 1707 it was decided that England and Scotland should have the same parliament. England, Wales and Scotland were now a United Kingdom.

◀ Highwaymen preyed upon travellers, holding up coaches and stealing valuables. Some, such as Dick Turpin (1706 to 1739), even became well-known figures.

In the 1700s

84 After Queen Anne died, the throne passed to kings from the German state of Hanover. The first four were all called George. They ruled Britain in the 1700s. By now there were two political parties called the Whigs and the Tories. From 1721 there was a prime minister, too.

86 Clever new machines were invented to spin yarn and weave cloth. They used water power or steam power. Machinery also helped on the farm. Jethro Tull invented a machine for sowing seed.

▼ Canals and new ways of farming changed the landscape of Britain in the 1700s. In fact farming changed so much, this time became known as the Agricultural Revolution.

85 Canals were built across the British Isles in the 1700s. They were dug out by gangs of workers called navigators or navvies. It was easier to carry goods on barges than on bumpy, muddy, winding roads.

87 People called Jacobites wanted to bring back Stuart rule. Many lived in Scotland and that was where two rebellions started. James Edward Stuart (son of James VII of Scotland/II of England) was defeated in 1715. In 1745 his son, Bonnie Prince Charlie, almost succeeded, but he was forced to flee the country after a grim defeat at Culloden in 1746.

▶ At the Battle of Culloden, the English Redcoats easily defeated the Scottish Jacobites.

The British Redcoats carried guns with bayonets (long blades attached to the end of their guns) – they attacked the Jacobites without mercy

The Scottish Jacobites wore uniforms of plaid and carried swords and shields – but they were no match for the Redcoats

Jethro Tull's seed drill

1700s QUIZ
1. What was a navvie?
2. What did Jethro Tull invent?
3. When was the Declaration of Independence drawn up?

Answers:
1. Navigator – a canal worker.
2. The seed drill. 3. 1776.

88 In the 1700s British traders and soldiers were seizing land all over the world. They fought with France to gain control of Canada and India. However in 1776, Britain began to lose control of its American colonies when the Declaration of Independence was drawn up. This recognized the right of the United States to break from British rule.

In the 1800s

89 Britain was at war with France from 1791 to 1802 and from 1803 to 1815. The British admiral Horatio Nelson won a great sea battle near Trafalgar, Spain, in 1805. From now on Britain's navy ruled the seas. In 1815 Sir Arthur Wellesley, who became Duke of Wellington, defeated the French Emperor Napoleon on land, at Waterloo in Belgium.

90 George III was old and going mad, so in 1811 his son was made Prince Regent to rule in his place. This Regency period was a time of high fashion. Elegant new buildings and parks were built. In 1820 the prince became king as George IV. He ruled over a United Kingdom that had, since 1801, included Ireland.

I DON'T BELIEVE IT!

Bathing in the sea became very popular at fashionable seaside towns. People were shy, so they changed in huts on wheels, called bathing machines. These were hauled into the waves. Some people said seawater was so good for you that they drank it!

91 After 1804, new clanking, puffing monsters disturbed the peace of the countryside. Great Britain built the world's first railways. At first, steam locomotives were used in mines, but by the 1830s trains carried passengers.

◄ The attempt by France to invade England failed at The Battle of Trafalgar. English cannons sank many French ships.

The Victorians

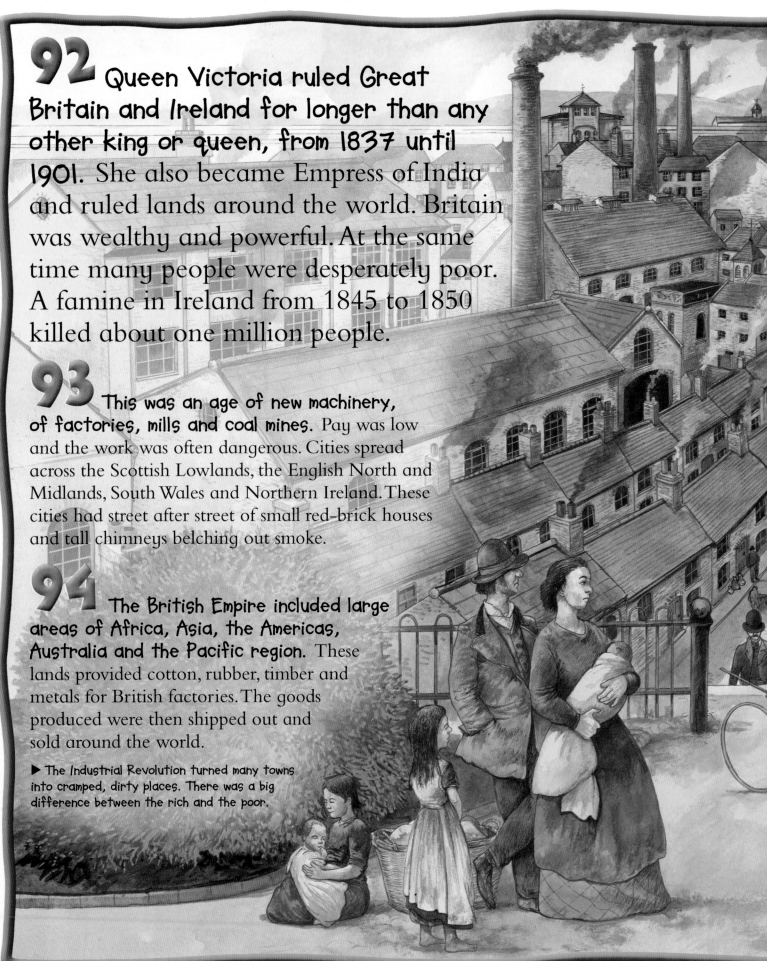

92 Queen Victoria ruled Great Britain and Ireland for longer than any other king or queen, from 1837 until 1901. She also became Empress of India and ruled lands around the world. Britain was wealthy and powerful. At the same time many people were desperately poor. A famine in Ireland from 1845 to 1850 killed about one million people.

93 This was an age of new machinery, of factories, mills and coal mines. Pay was low and the work was often dangerous. Cities spread across the Scottish Lowlands, the English North and Midlands, South Wales and Northern Ireland. These cities had street after street of small red–brick houses and tall chimneys belching out smoke.

94 The British Empire included large areas of Africa, Asia, the Americas, Australia and the Pacific region. These lands provided cotton, rubber, timber and metals for British factories. The goods produced were then shipped out and sold around the world.

▶ The Industrial Revolution turned many towns into cramped, dirty places. There was a big difference between the rich and the poor.

VICTORIAN PUNCH AND JUDY

Victorian children liked watching Punch and Judy puppet shows. Make these simple puppets and put on your own show.

You will need:

card scissors ice lolly sticks colouring pens

1. Draw the outlines of figures like the ones shown here onto card.

2. Colour them in then cut them out.

3. Stick an ice lolly stick to the back of each figure so that you can hold the puppets.

4. A sheet draped over two chairs can be your puppet theatre.

Punch

Policeman

Judy

45

The modern age

95 From 1914 to 1918 the nightmare of war spread around the world. In Europe, soldiers fought in the mud, pounded by guns. New weapons were used such as tanks and poison gas. Ten million soldiers died in this First World War.

◀ During the First World War, the *Sopwith Camel* became the most famous British fighter plane.

96 In 1916 there was a rising against British rule in Ireland. In the years that followed, most of Ireland broke away from the United Kingdom and became a separate country. Across the old empire, other peoples were demanding their freedom.

97 In the early 1900s women were marching and protesting. Men had won the right to vote in elections. Now these women, or suffragettes, wanted to do the same. In 1918 women over 30 were given the right to vote, and in 1928 women were given the same voting terms as men.

98 The 1920s and 1930s were a fun time for those who had money. There were motor cars, new dance crazes and jazz records. But many people had no work – and no money. Men from the town of Jarrow walked all the way from the northeast of England to London to protest at their hardship.

◀ Hunger marchers left Jarrow for London to raise awareness of the terrible unemployment in the northeast.

99 The Second World War took place from 1939 to 1945. Britain and many other countries fought against brutal governments that had come to power in Germany, Italy and Japan. It was the worst war in history and millions of innocent people were killed. Here, British and German fighter planes chase each other during the Battle of Britain in 1940.

100 Inventions changed everyone's lives in the 20th century. This was the age of the car, the ocean liner, the aeroplane and the space rocket. It was the age of films, videos, telephones and computers. This was the modern age.

▲ The Battle of Britain began in the late summer of 1940. By October, the British had won this battle for the skies.

Index